SLOVENI

TRAVEL GUIDE

2024

Your Comprehensive Travel Companion

for a Journey Beyond the Ordinary

CHARLES R. ERICKSON

Slovenia Travel Guide 2024

Copyright © 2024 Charles R. Erickson

Slovenia Travel Guide 2024

Table of Contents

Slovenia Travel Guide 2024

MAP OF SLOVENIA

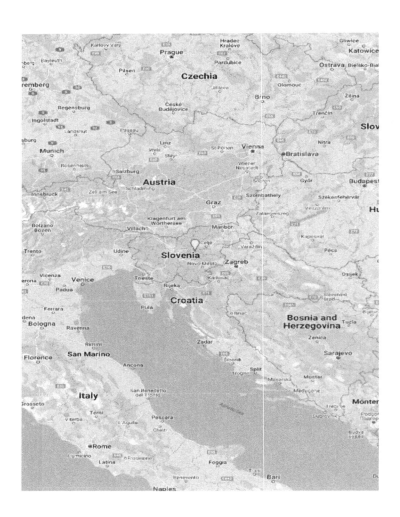

INTRODUCTION

Slovenia, an alluring nation with stunning scenery, a lively culture, and friendly people, lies tucked away between the Alps and the Adriatic Sea. Traveling to Slovenia is like traveling into a fantasy land, with emerald valleys dotted with quaint villages and glistening lakes reflecting the grandeur of snow-capped peaks. The picturesque capital of Slovenia, Ljubljana, is where my journey began. I was enthralled by the city's charming bridges, which were embellished with intricate ironwork and statuary, as soon as I started to meander along the Ljubljanica River. The Triple Bridge, a magnificent example of Baroque architecture, was a symbol of the city's cultural and historical legacy and stood proudly as the center of Ljubljana.

I left Ljubljana and went into the wild to discover the magical Lake Bled, a peaceful oasis in the middle of the Julian Alps. The lake's placid waters reflected the surrounding hills, and the charming island church—complete with a magnificent bell tower—brought a magical element to the setting.

I was astounded by the underground marvels of the Škocjan Caves, a UNESCO World Heritage Site, as I proceeded on my expedition. The enormous caves were whispered with the sounds of old geological processes and embellished with elaborate stalagmites and stalactites. I experienced a strong sense of connectedness to the planet's undiscovered wonders as I traveled deeper beneath the surface.

Without sampling some of Slovenia's delectable cuisine, no trip would be complete. I enjoyed the tastes of traditional Slovenian food, which included delicious pastries like potica, a sweet bread stuffed with raisins, almonds, and dried fruits, and hearty soups like goulash. Every mouthful was a harmonious blend of tastes, showcasing the nation's abundant farming legacy and gastronomic customs.

My trip to Slovenia was more than just a tour of the country's sights and flavors—it was an opportunity to see life at its core. I came across kind people who were excited to share their customs and tales. Their warm welcome and contagious energy created a striking image of Slovenia's rich cultural tapestry.

I set off on an adventure into the Julian Alps, a mecca for outdoor enthusiasts, leaving behind the urban beauty of Ljubljana. Hiking, cycling, and kayaking are all made more beautiful by the stunning scenery of the peaks, valleys, and lakes. I overcame the paths leading to the summit of Mount Triglav, the highest peak in Slovenia, within the Triglav National Park, the jewel in the crown of Slovenia. My arduous climb was rewarded with nothing short of amazing panoramic views at the top. I also went inside the Renaissance stronghold known as Predjama Castle, which is ominously poised on a rock. The already magical setting was made more mysterious by the castle's mysterious past, which is rich in legends of knights and wars.

CHAPTER ONE - GETTING TO KNOW THE SLOVENIA

Overview

Slovenia is a charming destination that offers a harmonious blend of natural beauty, cultural richness, and historical significance. It is a small country tucked between the Alps and the Adriatic Sea. Every traveler may find something to like in Slovenia, with its varied scenery, quaint villages, and friendly people.

Slovenia is a nation of opposites, with the Julian Alps dominating its northern region and a short but breathtaking Adriatic Sea shoreline adorning its western side. With their magnificent peaks, lush valleys, and glistening lakes, the Julian Alps are a haven for nature lovers who want to go hiking, cycling, or kayaking.

Slovenia Travel Guide 2024

On the other hand, Slovenia's southwest Karst area is home to a world of underground marvels. The area is well known for its unusual natural occurrences, underground caverns, and limestone formations. A must-see destination, Postojna Cave is a UNESCO World Heritage Site that features elaborate stalactites and stalagmites that have been sculpted by water over ages.

Slovenia's Slavic customs and surrounding countries' impacts are fundamental to the country's cultural legacy. The capital of the nation, Ljubljana, is a lovely city with a diverse architectural history that includes both modern and medieval constructions. Explore the cultural gems of Ljubljana with its pedestrian-friendly lanes packed with cafes, museums, and art galleries.

Slovenian culture is heavily reliant on customs and folklore. The nation is well-known for its colorful celebrations, like the Ljubljana Summer Festival and the Kurentovanje Carnival in Ptuj, as well as its folk dances, like the polka and waltz.

Slovenia Travel Guide 2024

Slovenian food is a delicious fusion of Mediterranean and Central European flavors. Fresh seafood dishes are popular along the shore, while hearty stews and savory goulashes are mainstays of Slovenian cuisine. The nation is particularly well-known for its pastries and sweets, such as prekmurska gibanica, a pastry stuffed with poppy seeds, apples, and walnuts, and potica, a tiered cake with a variety of fillings.

Slovenia is a year-round vacation spot with a range of sights and activities for every season. In the summer, the Adriatic coast beckons with its beaches and coastal town excursions, while the Julian Alps call with their hiking trails, cycling routes, and alpine lakes.

Autumn offers a brilliant display of fall foliage, and winter turns Slovenia into a snowshoeing, snowboarding, and skiing paradise. Festive Christmas markets abound in the nation's picturesque towns and cities, fostering a mystical ambiance. Slovenia is a great place for a quick trip or a longer journey because of its modest size, which makes exploration simple. Slovenia is a treasure in Central Europe that will enchant tourists with its varied landscapes, rich cultural legacy, and kind demeanor.

Geography and climate of Slovenia in Slovenia

Slovenia is a small nation with a tremendously varied climate and topography that provides visitors with a wide range of experiences. It is tucked away between the Alps and the Adriatic Sea. Slovenia's landscapes, which range from the sun-kissed Adriatic coast to the majestic Julian Alps, are a tribute to the craftsmanship of nature.

Geographic Variety: An Entire Tapestry of Scenes

Three separate regions make up Slovenia's geographical tapestry: the Pannonian Basin, the Alpine region, and the Dinaric region. Every area of the nation adds to its distinct personality and appeal.

The Alps: A World of Magnificent Peaks

For those who enjoy the great outdoors, the Julian Alps, a magnificent mountain range along Slovenia's northwest border, offer an amazing background. The tallest peak in Slovenia, Mount Triglav, is a source of pride for the country because of its sweeping vistas of the lakes and valleys below.

The Dinaric Area: A World of Karst Treasures

The most compelling natural features in Slovenia may be found in the Dinaric region, which is distinguished by its limestone structures and underground caves. With its elaborate stalactites and stalagmites, Postojna Cave is a UNESCO World Heritage Site that is a subterranean wonderland. The Predjama Castle, positioned precariously on a cliff face, lends the area a hint of medieval romance.

Pannonian Basin: A Region of Gently Sloping Hills and Wineries

The eastern portion of Slovenia is covered by the Pannonian Basin, which is characterized by mild slopes, lush plains, and vineyards. High-quality wines are produced here, including the well-known Zelen, a Sauvignon Blanc from the area, and the fragrant Pinot Noir.

Like its topography, Slovenia's climate varies greatly throughout its various areas. The Adriatic coast enjoys a Mediterranean climate with warm summers and moderate winters, whereas the Alpine region experiences a classic alpine environment with chilly winters and snowy peaks. The continental climate of the Dinaric region and the Pannonian Basin is characterized by scorching summers and chilly winters.

An Ice and Snow World in the Alps

The Julian Alps' Alpine climate is defined by chilly summers with nice temperatures and frigid winters with lots of snowfall. With skiing, snowboarding, and other winter sports available, this area is a winter sports enthusiast's dream come true.

Mediterranean Weather: A Sun-and-Sea World

Warm summers with clear skies and moderate winters with sporadic rainfall are characteristics of the Mediterranean climate found along the Adriatic coast. With its beaches, water activities, and relaxing by the sea, this area is a sun-lover's paradise.

Continental Weather: A Domain of Differing Seasons

The Dinaric region and Pannonian Basin have a continental climate, meaning that summers are hot and frequently reach temperatures in the mid-30s Celsius (90s Fahrenheit), while winters are frigid and frequently drop below freezing. This area is well-known for its agricultural output and vineyards.

Language and Culture in Slovenia

Slovenia is a fascinating nation that has historically absorbed influences from many different cultures. Situated amidst the Alps and the Adriatic Sea, Due to this blending, a rich cultural legacy was created, which is demonstrated by the varied languages spoken there, lively customs, and enthralling artwork.

An Ensemble of Customs

Slovenian culture has strong roots in Slavic customs that have been infused with elements from surrounding nations. At festivals and festivities, traditional folk dances like the polka and waltz are frequently seen, bringing a dynamic touch to the Slovenian character.

Slovenia

The nation is also home to distinctive traditions and rituals, like the colorful Kurentovanje Carnival in Ptuj, which features Kurenti, or costumed people, who ward off winter with their sheepskin outfits and bells.

A Refuge for Craftsmanship and Art

Slovenia has a rich and illustrious history of artistic and handicrafts, which is reflected in its folk art, architecture, and sculpture. Ljubljana, the capital city, is a veritable gold mine of architectural treasures, ranging from the baroque and medieval buildings to the contemporary constructions created by well-known architects.

Slovenian folk art is well known for its ceramics, vibrant fabrics, and dexterous wood carvings. Through the decades, these ancient crafts have been passed down, protecting the nation's cultural legacy and lending a sense of authenticity to its energetic cities and villages.

A Linguistic Landscape

With Slovene serving as the official language, Slovenia's linguistic environment is as varied as its cultural landscape. But because of its lengthy history, the nation has a bilingual population; some areas even speak Hungarian and Italian.

With its Slavic origins and influences from nearby languages, the Slovene language is an intriguing tongue with a distinctive syntax and sound. More than two million people speak the language globally, mostly in Slovenia but also in nearby nations and among Slovenian diaspora communities.

A Blend of Heritage and Modernity

Slovenia Travel Guide 2024

Slovenian culture is a well-balanced fusion of modern elements and traditional traditions. The nation has embraced modernity while preserving its beloved customs, artwork, and language. Slovenia's dynamic cultural landscape combines old-world elegance with modern vibrancy, making it an intriguing destination for tourists looking for a deep cultural experience.

CHAPTER TWO - GETTING READY

Visit Requirement

Schengen Area Citizens and Their Families: No Need for a Visa

For visits lasting up to 90 days within 180 days, citizens of the Schengen Area—which includes EU member states and several associated countries—do not need a visa. Regardless of their country, family members of Schengen Area citizens who are visiting Slovenia with or joining a Schengen Area citizen are likewise exempt from requiring a visa.

Visa Requirements for Citizens of Non-Schengen Areas

For visits to Slovenia, nationals of nations outside the Schengen Area often need to get a visa. The following paperwork must normally be submitted as part of the visa application process:

1. a valid passport that is at least three months past the planned stay in Slovenia and has two blank pages.

2. Two new passport-sized pictures.

an application for a visa that is filled out and signed.

3. Evidence of health insurance that will pay for medical costs during the trip.

4. Bank or credit card statements are examples of documentation attesting to the visitor's ability to sustain themselves throughout their visitation.

5. Evidence of lodging—a hotel reservation or an

An invitation from a Slovenian host should be provided.

6. Tickets for the entire journey or a confirmed schedule.

7. Further documentation can be needed, depending on the applicant's nationality and the particular visa category. It is best to find out the precise criteria that apply to your situation by contacting the appropriate Slovenian embassy or consulate.

Visa types and processing times

Tourist visas: Allow stays of up to 90 days throughout a 180-day period for short-term travel.

Visas for business travel are used for events like conferences and meetings.

Visas for transitory visitors: Those going through Slovenia on their way to another place.

Long-stay visas: Usually for employment, education, or family reunions, these visas allow stays longer than ninety days.

Application Procedures

Applications for visas may be filed in person at the appropriate Slovenian embassy or consulate in the applicant's home nation. As an alternative, applications may be sent by mail or via a recognized visa processing company.

- **Fees for visas:** These vary based on the applicant's nationality and the type of visa. Usually, fees must be paid at the time of application.

- **Biometric data collection:** As part of the visa application procedure, applicants may be asked to submit biometric information, such as a digital photo and their fingerprints.

- **Procedures for entry:** Passport and visa holders must be presented at the border crossing when they arrive in Slovenia. In addition, they can be asked to show proof of adequate funds and travel insurance.

The Best Time to Visit Slovenia

Slovenia is a year-round vacation spot with a range of sights and activities for every season. The ideal time to visit Slovenia, however, will depend on your tastes and areas of interest.

Summertime, from June to August

Slovenia's summer months are the best because of the pleasant, sunny weather that's perfect for outdoor pursuits like hiking, cycling, and kayaking. While the Adriatic shore provides chances for swimming, sunbathing, and water sports, the Julian Alps are an ideal place for climbing and mountaineering.

With festivals and events held all around the nation, summer is also a fantastic time to explore Slovenia's thriving cultural scene. One of the highlights of summer is the July and August Ljubljana Festival calendar, which presents a wide variety of acts, including opera, theater, and dance.

Shoulder Seasons: September to October and May to June

The shoulder seasons provide a more laid-back and reasonably priced option for the busy summer months. It is still a reasonable temperature for outdoor activities, with warm days and cold evenings. Additionally, there are fewer people there, so you can take in the sights in greater peace and quiet. Discover Slovenia's breathtaking scenery during the shoulder seasons, from the underground treasures of Postojna Cave to the lush slopes of the Julian Alps. Without the summertime throngs, you can take in the nation's rich cultural legacy by visiting galleries, museums, and historical sites.

Winter (November to April)

For lovers of winter sports, Slovenia becomes a winter wonderland in the winter months. While the quaint towns and villages hold lively Christmas markets and winter festivities, the Julian Alps are a refuge for skiers, snowboarders, and snowshoeing aficionados.

Slovenia's winter scenery is stunning, with snow-capped hills, frozen lakes, and quaint log cottages, even if you're not into winter sports. Indulge in luxurious treatments at the nation's thermal spas and wellness facilities to unwind after a day of experiencing the winter wonderland.

Parking tips in Slovenia

In general, parking in Slovenia is rather simple, and there are many options available for both short- and long-term parking. The following advice will help you manage Slovenia's parking scene:

Parking lot colors

▪ **Blue Zone:** These areas are frequently found in the heart of cities and are used for short-term parking, usually for between 30 and 2 hours. Parking must be paid for with a parking meter or a smartphone app.

- **Yellow Zone:** Yellow zones are designated for those who belong to particular categories, such as locals, people with disabilities, or cab drivers. To park in certain areas, a special permit is required.
- **White Zone:** Although there could be time constraints or other limitations, white zones are often free parking zones. Make sure you are not breaking any parking regulations by paying attention to the signage.

Mobile Apps and Parking Meters

In Slovenia, parking meters are commonplace, and they sometimes take credit cards in addition to coins. Convenient payment options for parking include using smartphone parking apps like ParkMe or EasyPark. With the help of these apps, you can remotely prolong your parking session without being overly polite.

Garages for parking

When looking for safe and practical parking, parking garages are a great choice, especially in urban areas. Usually, they charge by the hour, and you can pay with cash, credit card, or contactless payment methods as you leave.

Parking Advice for Particular Cities

▪ **Ljubljana:** There are several parking alternatives available in Ljubljana, including parking garages, park-and-ride facilities, and on-street parking. The city has an efficient parking system. If you're driving to the city center, you'll need to find parking outside of it because the city core is primarily pedestrianized.

▪ **Bled:** Because Bled is a well-liked tourist attraction, parking can be scarce, particularly in the summer. Think about parking at one of the approved lots along the lake or at Bled Castle.

▪ **Lake Bohinj:** There is plenty of parking near the lake and in the neighboring communities. Lake Bohinj is a peaceful location. If you want to go skiing or snowboarding, the Vogel Ski Center has parking available as well.

▪ **Postojna Cave:** Due to its popularity as a tourist destination, parking at Postojna Cave can get busy, particularly on weekends. Think about getting there early or parking at Predjama Castle, which is close by.

General Advice Regarding Parking

▪ **Observe parking signs:** To prevent fines or towing, always carefully read the parking signs.

▪ **Recognize parking zones:** Parking in the appropriate zone for your purposes is important because different zones have different laws and restrictions.
Utilize parking meters or smartphone apps. These practical ways let you pay for parking and remotely prolong your stay.

Think about parking garages. Particularly in urban areas, parking garages provide convenient and safe parking.

Remember the time constraints: Observe any time limits or other restrictions that are posted on parking signage.

Park sensibly. Refrain from obstructing traffic or parking in forbidden zones.

CHAPTER THREE - TOP DESTINATIONS IN SLOVENIA

Ljubljana

Slovenia Slovenia's capital, Ljubljana, is a dynamic and enchanting city tucked away in the Julian Alps' foothills. Known for its charming riverbank, medieval architecture, and vibrant arts and culture, Ljubljana is one of Europe's most alluring travel destinations.

Discovering the Soul of the City: Ljubljana Old Town

Wandering around Ljubljana's Old Town is like taking a trip back in time, with its cobblestone lanes winding past baroque churches and medieval houses. Situated on a hilltop with a commanding perspective of the city, the Ljubljana Castle provides panoramic vistas and an insight into the rich history of Slovenia.

The Dragon Bridge is a representation of the old traditions of Ljubljana, with its mythological creatures. The colorful Prešeren Square, the city's cultural center, can be reached by crossing the Ljubljanica River bridge. Here, street performers and lively cafes create an atmosphere that is contagious with vitality.

Gourmet Treats and a Charming Riverfront

The cuisine of Ljubljana is a fascinating fusion of international and traditional Slovenian dishes. Savor the flavor of goulash, indulge in hefty žlikrofi dumplings, or indulge in a slice of potica, a tiered cake stuffed with a variety of ingredients.

The Ljubljanica River, which flows through the heart of the city, brings some elegance and peace. Savor the picturesque scenery and the distinct viewpoint of the city from the water by taking a leisurely boat trip down the river.

Lake Bled

Lake Bled, a genuine gem of Slovenia, is tucked away amid the Julian Alps and features emerald waters, a lovely island, and a stunning backdrop of mountains and forests. This enchanting location is a well-liked option for tourists looking for a peaceful and enlightening escape because it provides a well-balanced combination of historical charm, natural beauty, and cultural attractions.

A Serene Lake with an Enchanting Island

The namesake island, which is the center of Lake Bled, is home to the Church of the Assumption, a serene and holy site dating back to the 17th century. The bell on the island, which has a melodic tone, is supposed to bring good fortune to those who ring it. Simply getting to the island is an adventure. Hire a rowboat to explore the lake at your own speed, or, for a more active experience, rent a traditional wooden pletna boat driven by an experienced gondolier.

A castle with a sweeping perspective

Bled Castle offers a stunning view of the surroundings from its perch atop a rock overlooking Lake Bled. The castle was first used as a fortification in the eleventh century, and it has since been used as a home, a museum, and more. For breathtaking views of the lake, the island, and the Julian Alps, climb the tower of the castle. Discover the rich history of the castle and see relics from many ages in the museum exhibits.

A Safe Haven for Outdoor Pursuits

Those looking for adventure and leisure can engage in a range of outdoor activities around Lake Bled. Enjoy a beautiful bike ride or trek around the lake. savoring the beautiful scenery and clean air. Take a stand-up paddleboard or kayak rental and enjoy cruising the calm waters of the lake. Try swimming in the lake's cool waters for a more thrilling experience, or go farther to explore the neighboring mountains.

A Haven of Taste

Savor the delicious food that Lake Bled has to offer. Taste the classic kremšnita, a custard cake with whipped cream on top, or sample the potica, a tiered cake with a variety of savory or sweet ingredients. Try the savory goulash, which is a stew of meat, vegetables, and spices, or a dish of žlikrofi, which are dumplings filled with meat or potatoes, for a heartier supper.

Piran

The village of Piran is enthralling, radiating a distinct fusion of Mediterranean beauty and Venetian charm. Piran, one of Slovenia's most charming and attractive towns, has gained recognition for its charming cobblestone alleys, old buildings, and lively atmosphere.

Traveling Back in Time: Seeing the Old Town

Explore Piran's Old Town, a maze of winding alleyways dotted with buildings in the Venetian style, and feel like you've stepped back in time. See the exquisite features of the Tartini area, which bears the name of the famous violinist Giuseppe Tartini, and take in the vibrant atmosphere of the stores and cafés that line the area.

Explore the magnificent Baroque St. George's Cathedral and go to the summit of its bell tower for awe-inspiring sweeping views of the town, the Adriatic Sea, and the far-off Julian Alps.

An enormous art and cultural treasure

Piran, with its many museums and galleries exhibiting the town's rich history and innovative spirit, is a sanctuary for lovers of art and culture. Explore the town's cultural heritage at the Giuseppe Tartini Music Museum, or lose yourself in the world of nautical history at the nautical museum of Piran. Visit the Piran Coastal Galleries for a taste of contemporary art; there, alternating displays feature pieces by regional and foreign artists.

Gourmet Treats by the Sea

The food scene in Piran is as varied as its past, featuring a delicious blend of Mediterranean and Slovenian flavors. Savor the flavors of authentic Slovenian food, indulge in fresh fish dishes, or reward yourself with a slice of Prekmurska gibanica, a layered pastry stuffed with walnuts, apples, and poppy seeds.

A Safe Haven for Pleasure and Entertainment

For those looking to unwind and have fun, Piran has a wide range of possibilities. Take a leisurely stroll around the town's beaches and enjoy the warmth of the sun.

Promenade or venture into the nearby countryside to explore the scenic hiking trails and cycling routes. In the evenings, immerse yourself in the town's lively atmosphere, with music and entertainment filling the streets and squares. Enjoy a traditional Slovenian folk music performance or soak up the sounds of jazz or classical music at one of Piran's many venues.

Triglav National Park

Slovenia has only one national park, Triglav, which is an amazing wonderland of towering hills, verdant valleys, and crystal-clear lakes. This untouched wilderness, which makes up about 4% of Slovenia's geographical area, is a paradise for outdoor explorers, nature lovers, and anybody looking for a peaceful getaway amid the stunning alpine scenery.

A World of Towering Peaks and Wilderness Untamed

Mount Triglav, the park's namesake, is a symbol of Slovenian pride, rising to a remarkable 2,864 meters (9,396 feet) above sea level on its top. From its towering heights, expansive vistas spread out before you, displaying a mosaic of lush valleys, crystal-clear lakes, and the far-off silhouettes of nearby peaks.

A Paradise for Hikers and Outdoor Enthusiasts

With a network of routes crisscrossing its varied landscapes, Triglav National Park is a hiker's dream destination. While less demanding treks give wonderful views and chances to connect with the peace of nature, more experienced climbers can test their mettle on the ascent to Mount Triglav. The park's forested areas and alpine meadows are home to chamois, golden eagles, and even the elusive brown bear. As you stroll the park's trails, keep an eye out and an ear out for the sounds of nature's orchestra.

A Symphony of Lakes and Enchanting Waters

There is a captivating assortment of lakes in Triglav National Park, each with its own distinct personality and allure. Lake Bled is a well-liked location for leisurely strolls and boat cruises because of its charming island and medieval castle.

While Lake Jasna, tucked away on the Pokljuka Plateau, is a refuge for seclusion and unspoiled beauty, Lake Bohinj, set amid peaceful forests, offers a peaceful getaway.

A Multicultural Tapestry Incorporated into the Scenere

The ancient settlements and dispersed homesteads that adorn the valleys of Triglav National Park provide witness to the park's rich cultural legacy. See the continuing traditions of alpine farming by visiting the shepherd's huts, or "planšarje," and indulge in the regional specialties, including the filling žlikrofi dumplings and the sweet Prekmurska gibanica pastry.

Škocjan Caves

Situated in Slovenia's Karst area, the Škocjan Caves are among the world's most remarkable cave systems and a UNESCO World Heritage Site. The caverns are renowned for their striking natural features, which include immense cave halls, subterranean rivers, and towering waterfalls. They are home to a vast network of underground tubes, chambers, and canyons.

An Exploration of the Interior of the Earth

The limestone at the Škocjan Caves was dissolved by subterranean water. The water has chiseled away a massive network of tunnels and chambers over millions of years, some reaching heights of up to 140 meters (460 feet).

The Upper Cave and the Lower Cave are the two primary divisions of the caves. A guided tour is available to visit the Upper Cave, which is home to several breathtaking rock formations, such as the Great Canyon, a 140-meter (460-foot) deep canyon with a tumbling waterfall.

The Martel Cave, the largest underground canyon in the world, is located in the Lower Cave, which is only accessible by guided tour. There is an underground river in the 250-meter (820-foot)-deep Martel Cave that may flow at a speed of up to 100 liters per second (26 gallons per second).

A Home to a Diverse Ecosystem

Slovenia Travel Guide 2024

A rich ecology with a wide range of flora and fauna can be found in the Škocjan Caves. In addition to cave crickets, beetles, and spiders, the caves are home to more than 100 different kinds of bats. A wide range of flora, including ferns, wildflowers, and mosses, can be found in the caverns.

A well-liked vacation spot

The Škocjan Caves are a well-liked tourist spot that draws people from all over the world. Year-round public access to the caves is offered, with guided tours offered in Slovenian, German, Italian, and English.

Tips for Visiting the Škocjan Caves

The pleasant weather in the spring and fall makes these seasons the ideal times to visit the Škocjan Caves.

Select comfy shoes, as you will be walking a lot in them.

CHAPTER FOUR - ACTIVITIES AND EXPERIENCE IN SLOVENIA

Hiking and Outdoor Activities

Lake Bled: Take a leisurely stroll around the lake's edge and enjoy the scenic vistas of the island and Bled Castle.

Vintgar Gorge: Explore the Radovna River's sculpted Vintgar Gorge, a natural wonder, and take in the lush foliage and waterfalls.

Triglav National Park: Take a hike up Slovenia's highest peak, Mount Triglav, or take one of the park's many other paths through a variety of scenic settings.

Cycle Routes for Stunning Tours

Bohinj Valley: Ride a bicycle through this serene valley that is surrounded by the Julian Alps and features immaculate lakes, verdant meadows, and a serene setting.

Soča Valley: Take a leisurely bicycle ride through this picturesque valley, renowned for its emerald river, quaint villages, and majestic mountains.

Parenzana Trail: Take a ride along this former railroad track that has been transformed into a bike route with breathtaking views of the Adriatic shore.

Adventures in Water Sports

Kayaking in Lake Bled: Experience Lake Bled's serene waters from a different angle while admiring the lovely island and Bled Castle.

The Soča River is a well-known site for whitewater rafting. Venture through its rapids and enjoy the exhilaration of the river's currents.

Lake Bohinj stand-up Paddleboarding: Take in the breathtaking mountain views while having a relaxed stand-up paddleboarding experience on this beautiful lake.

- **Wintertime Excursions** Julian Alps skiing and snowboarding: Experience the exhilaration of sliding down snow-covered mountains at Slovenia's top ski areas, like Kranjska Gora and Krvavec.

▪ **Snowshoeing and Cross-Country Skiing:** Take a snowshoe or cross-country ski trip through Slovenia's natural woods and national parks to experience the peaceful wintertime ambiance.

▪ **Ice Skating and Ice Climbing:** Take on new challenges by going ice skating on frozen lakes or ice climbing in the Julian Alps.

Culinary Delights

Hearty Slovenian staples

Slovenia's robust meals, handed down through the years, represent the country's rich history and cultural legacy. Savor the flavor of goulash, a delightful stew of meat, veggies, and spices, or indulge in žlikrofi, delicate dumplings filled with meat or potatoes.

Fresh seafood appetizers

Fresh fish is the main feature of the Adriatic coast. Savor the delicate flavors of scampi, grill some squid, or have a bowl of classic fish stew, brodetto.

Slovenia Travel Guide 2024

Delightful Treats and Customary Pastries

Desserts are another aspect of Slovenian culinary traditions, offering a wide range of confections to entice your palate. Try the whipped cream-topped custard cake, kremšnita, or indulge in the layered tastes of potica, a pastry stuffed with walnuts, apples, or poppy seeds.

Local Culinary Treasures

Slovenian regions are proud of their unique gastronomic offerings. Savor Prekmurska gibanica, a layered cake with a special blend of savory and sweet contents, while visiting the Prekmurje region. Sample pršut, a prosciutto-like dry-cured ham, and savor the flavorful jota, a hearty soup with beans, cabbage, and pork, both from the Karst area.

Regional wines and drinks

The wine-producing regions of Slovenia produce a wide range of superb wines, including strong reds and crisp whites. Savor the deep flavors of Merlot and Cabernet Sauvignon from the Posavje region, or sample the well-known white wine Rebula from the

Primorska region. Try bezg, a classic elderflower cordial, or sip on a glass of toplar, a sparkling grape juice, for a pleasant drink.

Events and cultural festivals

Summertime Celebrations: An Orchestra of Song, Painting, and Tradition

In Slovenia, the summer months are when the most festivals take place all around the nation. Experience the lively atmosphere of the world-famous Ljubljana Festival, which features a wide variety of acts ranging from modern theater to classical music. Accept the customary mindset of Kurentovanje is a Ptuj carnival where participants don colorful costumes and perform energetic dances to ward off winter spirits.

Fall Favorites: Snacking Events and Creative Creations

Slovenia has an abundance of food festivals and creative manifestations throughout the fall. Savor the flavors of Slovenia's varied cuisine at the Radovljica Festival of Taste, where regional chefs present their dishes. At the Slovenian Book Fair in Ljubljana, which brings together writers, publishers, and readers, you can immerse yourself in the world of literature, discover new works, and interact with the literary community.

Festive Markets and Cultural Events During the Winter Season

Slovenia becomes a world of merry markets and cultural events come wintertime. Wander around the charming Christmas markets in Bled, Ljubljana, and other towns, which are decorated with traditional crafts, glowing lights, and the aroma of delectable holiday foods.

Children anticipate the advent of the kind saint on St. Nicholas Day, which is celebrated throughout Slovenia. Warm up with traditional mulled wine and savor festive treats.

Water Sport

Canoeing and kayaking: Slovenia is a great place to go canoeing and kayaking because of its network of peaceful lakes and meandering rivers. Sail over the emerald waters of Lake Bled, which is encircled by scenic mountains and Bled Castle, or discover the Soča Valley, renowned for its glistening river and breathtaking vistas.

▪ **Whitewater Rafting:** Savor the excitement of this thrilling activity on the Soča River, a globally recognized attraction. Experience the surge of excitement as you face the challenges presented by the river's currents as you navigate its rapids, which are surrounded by towering peaks and rich foliage.

▪ **Get up Paddleboarding:** Take in the peace and quiet of Slovenia's rivers and lakes while stand-up paddling. Canoe the coastlines of Visit Lake Bohinj, which is encircled by the striking Julian Alps, or venture into the Adriatic coast's undiscovered bays and inlets.

▪ **cruising:** Sail over the Adriatic Sea's azure seas to discover Slovenia's stunning coastline and quaint coastal towns. Sail lazily and take in the breathtaking vistas of the sea, or experience the exhilaration of windsurfing, where you use the wind's power to maneuver the waves.

- **Snorkeling and diving:** Explore Slovenia's glistening lakes and the Adriatic Sea's underwater habitat. Snorkeling or diving will allow you to see the vivid coral reefs, abundant marine life, and secret underwater caverns.

CHAPTER FIVE
TRANSPORTATION

Getting Around Slovenia

- **Boutique Hotels:** A Smidge of Personality and Charm Slovenia's boutique hotels offer a charming haven for individuals looking for a customized and private stay. These tiny, independently run businesses have a distinct charm and personality that frequently reflect the local culture and ambience.

- **Hotel Triglav Bled:** Located on the beaches of Lake Bled, this little hotel offers breathtaking views of Bled Castle and the lake while combining classic elegance and contemporary comfort. Situated in the center of Ljubljana's Old Town, Hotel Heritage Ljubljana is a boutique hotel that offers an opulent and culturally absorbing stay by skillfully fusing modern and traditional architectural elements.

- **Venturing by bus:** Slovenia's bus network links rural communities, smaller cities, and outlying areas to the rail network. Because they offer frequent connections and affordable fares, buses are an effective means of seeing the many regions of the nation.

- **Driving on Slovenian Roads:** Slovenia's well-maintained road network makes it simple to reach major locations and attractions. Highways connect major cities, and picturesque minor roads wind across breathtaking landscapes. To drive on Slovenian motorways, one must get a vignette, a sticker that allows unlimited use of the roads for a pre-arranged period of time.

- **Cycling for a Scenic Adventure:** Slovenia's varied topography and well-maintained bike lanes make it a cyclist's paradise. Explore the quaint Soča Valley, cycle along the perimeter of Lake Bled, or go into the Julian Alps to enjoy the breathtaking views and tranquility of the wilderness.

- **Boat Travel:** Slovenia offers options for boat travel around the country thanks to its numerous lakes and the Adriatic Sea. You can take a boat tour of Lake Bled, rent a kayak or canoe to find hidden coves and inlets, or use a ferry to get from one coastal town to another.

▪ **Cities:** Slovenia's major cities, including Maribor, Koper, and Ljubljana, have efficient public transportation systems. The bus or tram, which links several parts of the city, is a convenient and affordable way to get around. For quick excursions, consider hiring a bike or taking a walking tour of the city to see its charming streets and vibrant atmosphere.

Public Transportation:

▪ **Exploring Slovenia's Scenic Routes:** Run by Slovenske železnice (Sž), the country's railway operator, the rail network connects major cities and towns throughout Slovenia and covers a distance of about 1,200 kilometers (745 miles). Train travel is a delightful experience that takes you past historic castles, through breathtaking landscapes, and along the Adriatic coast.

- **Buses: Traveling to Slovenia's Heart** In addition to the train system, Slovenia's extensive bus network provides connectivity to smaller towns and cities as well as remote locations. Buses offer frequent connections and affordable costs, making them an easy method to get about the country's various regions, from the serene countryside to the energetic capital.

- **Urban Mobility:** Navigating Slovenia's Cities Within their metropolitan regions, Slovenia's major cities—Maribor, Koper, and Ljubljana—have efficient public transportation systems. A cost-effective and useful mode of transit in the city are the bus, tram, and even the funicular systems that connect various locations. By renting a bicycle or taking short walks, you can easily explore the vibrant atmosphere and charming streets of these fascinating cities.

Ticketing and Fare Options

Slovenia's public transport system uses a zonal fare structure, with fares determined by the number of zones traversed. Bus drivers themselves, ticket kiosks, and ticket machines sell tickets. If you travel frequently, you might wish to purchase a travel pass, such as the Ljubljana Urbana Card, which offers convenient access to a range of affordable public transportation options.

Passenger comfort and accessibility

Slovenia's public transport network will provide comfortable and accessible travel for all passengers. Most train stations and bus stops have ramps and elevators, and many buses and trams have low floors for easy boarding. Passengers with impairments are provided with specific seating and have the option to request assistance.

Driving Tips

1. Driving Laws and Regulations: Become acquainted with Slovenia's driving laws and regulations before your departure. Observing the posted speed limits is one of them; these are typically 50 km/h (31 mph) in urban areas, 110 km/h (68 mph) on major thoroughfares, and 130 km/h (81 mph) on highways. They also include constantly using your headlights and staying on the right side of the road.

2. Important documents: Always keep your driver's license, insurance certificate, and car registration documents current when driving in Slovenia. During traffic inspections, police officers could request certain documents.

3. Essential Equipment: Ensure that your vehicle has the necessities, including extra bulbs for your outside lights, a warning triangle, and a first aid kit. You may require headlamp converters if your headlights are not configured for right-side driving.

Seatbelt usage and child safety: Both front and rear passengers are required to buckle up. Children younger than twelve must use appropriate child safety restraints, such as booster seats or car seats.

4. Use of Cell Phones: Avoid using portable cell phones while driving. While it's legal to use a hands-free device while driving, it's best to minimize distractions.

Alcohol Consumption: The legal limit for drivers in Slovenia is 0.05% of blood. If you wish to drive, it's best to entirely refrain from alcohol.

5. Road Signage and Conditions: Be prepared for shifting conditions on the roadways, especially when passing through hilly areas or during bad weather. It is important to pay attention to road signs and markings, which are usually posted in both Slovenian and English.

6. Parking laws: Acquaint yourself with the rules governing parking in various locations. Keep an eye out for parking lots that are well marked, and be mindful of any time limits and associated costs.

Emergency Assistance: In the event of an emergency, dial 112, the European emergency number, to get in touch with the appropriate emergency services, such as the police, ambulance, or fire department.

CHAPTER SIX - ACCOMMODATIONS IN SLOVENIA

Hotels and Resorts

1. Boutique Hotels: A Smidge of Personality and Charm

Slovenia's boutique hotels offer a charming haven for individuals looking for a customized and private stay. These tiny, independently run businesses have a distinct charm and personality that frequently reflect the local culture and ambience.

2. Hotel Triglav Bled: Located on the beaches of Lake Bled, this little hotel offers breathtaking views of Bled Castle and the lake while combining classic elegance and contemporary comfort.

Situated in the center of Ljubljana's Old Town, Hotel Heritage Ljubljana is a boutique hotel that offers an opulent and culturally absorbing stay by skillfully fusing modern and traditional architectural elements.

3. Hotel & Restaurant Jezero Bohinj: This charming hotel provides a calm haven amidst stunning natural beauty. It is located on the quiet beaches of Lake Bohinj. The hotel's restaurant offers mouthwatering regional fare and stunning views of the lake.

4. Hotel Vila Planinka: This boutique hotel offers a refuge of rustic charm and alpine ambience, nestled in the charming village of Kransjka Gora. The hotel's wellness facility has a variety of relaxing treatments that are ideal for a restorative getaway.

5. Luxurious Resorts: Indulging and Rewarding Amid the Magnificence of Nature

Slovenia's upscale resorts take the hospitality industry to new levels by providing top-notch amenities, flawless service, and an environment of unparalleled scenic beauty. These resorts are ideal for anyone looking for an opulent getaway amidst magnificent scenery.

6. Kempinski Palace Portoroz: This lavish resort, which is perched on a cliffside with views of the Adriatic Sea, combines contemporary luxury with Venetian-inspired architecture. Gourmet cuisine, a top-notch spa, and exclusive beach access are available to guests.

7. The Grand Hotel Toplice: This venerable resort has been serving guests since 1910 and is situated in the spa town of Dolenjske Toplice. The hotel's wellness programs, saunas, and thermal baths offer a sanctuary of rest and renewal.

8. Hotel Sotelia: This opulent resort provides a comprehensive wellness experience and is nestled in the peaceful surroundings of Terme Olimia. Surrounded by lush nature, guests can enjoy a range of spa treatments, saunas, and thermal pools.

9. LifeClass Hotels & Spa: Offering a variety of opulent lodging options and wellness amenities, LifeClass Hotels & Spa has several locations around Slovenia. In breathtaking natural settings, guests can enjoy hot pools, saunas, exercise centers, and fine cuisine.

Hotels and resorts in Slovenia serve a diverse array of guests, from those looking for secluded, enchanting getaways to those desiring opulent luxury amidst stunning landscapes. Whether you're drawn to the lavish atmosphere of luxury resorts or the rustic appeal of boutique hotels, Slovenia provides a singular and remarkable hospitality experience.

Hotels and Budget Stays in Slovenia

- **Low-Cost Hostels:** A Social and Economic Choice
Slovenia's hostels offer a cozy and friendly environment for visitors looking for a cheap and social place to stay. There are several shared dorm rooms available at these hostels.
- **Celica Hostel in Ljubljana:** This unique hostel offers a blend of history and contemporary convenience, housed in a former prison that has been transformed into a cultural center. There are

several common areas for visitors to enjoy, such as a bar, café, and co-working space.

▪ **Hostel Tresor Maribor:** Conveniently located in the center of Maribor, this hostel offers a cozy and welcoming base for discovering the city. The hotel's café and bar provide a vibrant environment, and visitors may take part in a range of planned events and activities.

The cozy Hostel Kekec Kranjska Gora is situated in the charming village of Kranjska Gora and offers a warm and inviting environment. The personnel at the hotel can help plan trips and outdoor activities.

Cheap Hotels and Vacation Rentals: Coziness and Economy Slovenia has a range of reasonably priced hotels and guest homes that are ideal for travelers looking for a comfy and affordable option. These accommodations frequently offer private rooms with minimal amenities, which makes them an affordable choice for tourists on a tight budget.

Located in the city's center, Hotel Center Ljubljana is a reasonably priced lodging option that provides cozy surroundings and an ideal starting point for city exploration. The professional and kind personnel at the hotel may have ideas for places to eat and see.

The family-run Guest House Pr'Gavedina Bohinj is a warm and inviting place to stay, tucked away in the peaceful surroundings of Lake Bohinj. The guest home offers breathtaking views of the surrounding mountains and the lake, along with delectable local cuisine.

▪ **Hotel Maj Bovec:** This budget hotel offers a cozy starting point for exploring the Soča Valley and is situated in the charming town of Bovec. The hotel offers a range of outdoor activities, including hiking, bicycling, and rafting, in addition to serving up hearty local cuisine in the restaurant.

Nestled in the picturesque town of Brežice, Guest House Pr'Mlinar Brežice provides a peaceful haven amidst Posavje's undulating hills. Traditional Slovenian cuisine is served at the guest house's restaurant, and visitors can engage in a range of outdoor pursuits like hiking, cycling, and kayaking.

Unique Accommodation Options in Slovenia

1 Camping in the Bosom of Nature

Get lost in the peaceful splendor of the Slovenian countryside by choosing glamping, an opulent kind of camping that mixes the excitement of being outside with the amenities of a hotel. There are many glamping locations around the nation that provide a range of lodging options, including comfortable yurts and treehouses, as well as roomy tents with luxurious mattresses.

- **Glamping Ribno:** This glamping location provides a tranquil getaway amidst the verdant surroundings of Ribno. There is a communal grill area, outdoor terraces, and private tents with private restrooms.

- **Hija Glamping Lake Bloke:** This glamping location, which lies on the lake's edge, offers a peaceful environment for adventure and relaxation. There are other glamping alternatives available to visitors, such as tents. With panoramic views, as well as enjoy a range of outdoor activities, such as hiking, biking, and kayaking.

Situated in the center of the Velika Planina plateau, the eco-friendly camping resort Eko resort pod Veliko Planino provides a distinctive fusion of contemporary comfort and rustic charm. During their visit, guests can take advantage of the sauna, bike trails, and children's playground at the resort, which is designed to resemble ancient shepherds' huts.

2. **Vineyard Cottages:** Slovenian Terroir Revealed

A zidanica is a traditional grape hut where you can stay and enjoy the charm of Slovenia's wine regions. Originally employed as product storage by wineries, these rustic stone buildings today provide a distinctive and genuine lodging choice.

▪ **Zidanica Brdo:** Tucked away among the Vipava Valley's vineyards, this quaint zidanica gives a flavor of regional winemaking customs. Visitors can savor the host's handmade wine and regional specialties on the private patio, which offers breathtaking views of the valley.

- **Zidanica Klinec:** Nestled amid vineyards and rolling hills, this classic zidanica offers a peaceful haven in the charming village of Šmartno pri Slovenj Gradcu. Visitors can take advantage of a private garden with grilling amenities and go on bike or foot excursions around the neighboring countryside.

- **Zidanica Pri Grapih:** This rustic zidanica provides a warm and genuine experience, and it is located in the center of the Maribor wine area. In addition to taking part in wine tastings and learning about regional winemaking methods, guests can savor a traditional fireplace.

3. Farmstead Stays: An Intimacy with Country Living

Staying on a working farm will allow you to fully experience Slovenia's rural traditions. These farmstead stays give visitors a chance to witness real rural life and provide a window into the agricultural history of the nation.

- **Tourist Farm Pr'Gavedina:** This family-run farmstead provides a cozy and inviting ambiance, nestled in the serene surroundings of Lake Bohinj. In addition to participating in farm activities and learning about local culture, guests can savor traditional Slovenian food.

▪ **Tourist Farm Klinar:** This traditional farmstead offers a taste of rural Slovenian life and is situated in the charming village of Podkum. A range of farm-to-table cuisine is served, and visitors can engage in outdoor pursuits like cycling, hiking, and horseback riding.

▪ **Tourist Farm Firšt:** This family-run farmstead offers a distinctive fusion of modern comfort and history, and it is located in the center of the Pohorje area. Along with taking part in agricultural activities and tasting regional cuisine, guests can relax in a private apartment with a balcony and breathtaking views of the mountains.

CHAPTER SEVEN LOCAL CUISINE AND DINING IN SLOVENIA

Traditional Slovenian Dishes

1. Štruklji: Doughnut Rolls

A mainstay of Slovenian cuisine, Štruklji comes in different variations depending on the area. These adaptable dumplings are a popular option for both main meals and desserts because they can be filled with savory or sweet ingredients.

- **Savory Štruklji:** A filling and fulfilling dish, savory štruklji are packed with a blend of meat, potatoes, onions, and herbs. Usually, cracklings or a dollop of sour cream are placed on top of them.

- **Sweet Štruklji:** A delicious contrast to their savory siblings, these dumplings are stuffed with sweet ingredients such as poppy seeds, apples, or cottage cheese. Sweet štruklji are frequently served with a honey drizzle or a coating of powdered sugar.

2. fganci: spoonbread or cornmeal

A thick porridge-like consistency is achieved by cooking cornmeal in water or milk to make Žganci, a versatile food. It's a hearty and satisfying dish that's typically served with cracklings, sour cream, or a flavorful stew.

- **Buckwheat Ganci:** This type of Žganci has a heartier texture and a slightly nutty flavor, as it is made with buckwheat flour. It is frequently served with goulash or sautéed mushrooms.

- **Corn Žganci:** Made with cornmeal, this traditional Žganci has a mild flavor and a smooth, creamy texture. It goes nicely with many other kinds of toppings, such as sausages and stews, as well as cracklings and sour cream.

3. Potica: Rolled Dough Slovenian Cake

Potica is a classic Slovenian pastry made with a variety of savory or sweet contents wound around a thin, fragile dough. It's a favorite dessert for holidays and special events, and there are regional varieties to enjoy.

Walnut Potica: The most well-known and traditional potica variant, it has a sweet and nutty walnut filling. Spices and honey are common flavors for the walnut filling.

Poppy Seed Potica: Another well-liked choice, poppy seed potica has an earthy, sweet filling consisting of milk, sugar, and powdered poppy seeds. It can also be seasoned with cloves and cinnamon.

Cheese Potica: Packed with a creamy blend of cottage cheese, eggs, and herbs, cheese potica is a savory option. It's frequently offered as a little meal or snack.

4. Kremna Rezina: Custard Cake

The rich delicacy known as kremna rezina has come to represent Slovenian pastry making. It has three layers: a thick custard filling, a layer of thin dough, and a vanilla sugar and whipped cream topping.

- **Classic Kremna Rezina:** The classic kremna rezina has a layer of whipped cream on top and a thin dough that reveals the custard inside, giving it an exquisite yet simple presentation.

- **Chocolate Kremna Rezina:** A rich and luscious take on the traditional dessert, this version has a layer of dark chocolate mousse sandwiched between the whipped cream and the custard filling.

- **Fruit Kremna Rezina:** A light and tasty dessert, fruit kremna rezina adds sliced fruits or fresh berries to the custard mixture for a cool variation.

5. Carniolan sausage, or Kranjska Klobasa

Slovenia's well-known cured pork product, Kranjska klobasa, comes from the Carniola region. It is a tasty and flavorful sausage produced from a mixture of pork, beef, and spices that is expertly smoked.

- **Grilled Kranjska Klobasa:** Traditionally, Kranjska klobasa is eaten by grilling it until the flesh is thoroughly cooked and the skin is crispy. It is frequently served with mashed potatoes, a side salad, or sauerkraut.

Chunks of Kranjska klobasa are cooked in a flavorful tomato-based sauce together with veggies and seasonings in this filling stew. This dish is hearty and filling, ideal for a chilly winter's day.

- **Kranjska Klobasa Salad:** This light and refreshing dish blends the savory sausage with fresh vegetables, mixed greens, and a vinaigrette dressing. This tasty and healthful recipe highlights Kranjska klobasa's versatility.

Must-Try Restaurants and Cafes

1. **Hiša Franko**, located in Kobarid, is a Michelin-starred restaurant known for its inventive and sustainable take on Slovenian cuisine. It is tucked away in the stunning Soča Valley. Pioneer of modern Slovenian cuisine, Chef Ana Roš creates visually appealing and flavor-bursting dishes using ingredients gathered locally.

2. **JB Restaurant, Ljubljana:** This chic, modern restaurant provides a classy dining experience and is situated in the center of Ljubljana's Old Town. The restaurant's menu features contemporary Slovenian cooking that emphasizes using fresh,

in-season ingredients and creative presentation techniques.

3. **Strelec, Ljubljana:** Located atop Ljubljana Castle, Strelec serves up classic Slovenian fare with a contemporary touch and provides expansive city views. Fresh, regional ingredients are used to prepare a wide selection of meats, cheeses, and seasonal vegetables on the restaurant's menu.

4. **Pri Lojzetu, Vipava Valley:** This family-run restaurant has been dishing up traditional Slovenian food for generations, and it is tucked away among the vineyards and undulating hills of the Vipava Valley. The restaurant's menu highlights classic meals created using ingredients that are sourced locally, showcasing the area's rich culinary legacy.

5. **Pr'Speh, Bled:** Perched on the edge of Lake Bled, Pr'Speh provides a distinctive dining experience accompanied by breathtaking views of Bled Castle and the lake. Fresh, in-season ingredients are used to construct a menu that

combines both foreign and traditional Slovenian meals.

6. Kavarna Zvezda, Ljubljana: Visit this quaint café in the Central Market of Ljubljana for a sample of classic Slovenian coffee culture. Since 1952, this storied café has been providing delicious pastries and freshly roasted coffee.

7. Authentic Slovenian pastries and desserts have been served at Trubarjeva Hiša, a pleasant and historic café located in the heart of Ljubljana's Old Town, for over a century. The Prekmurska gibanica, a tiered cake stuffed with poppy seeds, apples, walnuts, and cottage cheese, is the café's specialty dish.

8. Literarna kavarna Lolita, Maribor: This lively café in the city's historic center acts as a gathering place for writers and artists from the area. In addition to a selection of coffees, teas, and light fare, the café has a homey feel with a hint of literary appeal.

9. Kavarna Liza, Piran: Located on the charming shoreline in Piran, Kavarna Liza provides a pleasant environment for sipping coffee or a cool beverage. Admire breathtaking views of the Adriatic Sea and the ancient city walls from the café's outdoor terrace.

10. Kavarna Park, Maribor: Situated amidst the lush surroundings of City Park in Maribor, Kavarna Park is a well-liked location for both locals and tourists. In addition to providing a large assortment of coffees, teas, and refreshments, the café has a laid-back vibe.

CHAPTER EIGHT - LANGUAGE AND CULTURE IN SLOVENIA

Basic Slovenian Phrases

Greetings and Essentials

Hi there, I'm Živjo (ZHEE-vyoh) or Zdravo (ZDRAH-vo).

Good day, dober dan (DOH-ber dahn).

Good morning, dobro jutro (DOH-broh YOO-troh).

Good evening, or dober večer (DOH-ber VECH-ehr).

Good night, Lahko noč (LAH-ko noch).

Hvala / HVAL-ah / I'm grateful

Please, Prosim (PROH-seem)

Please pardon me, Oprostite (OH-proh-stee-teh).

Neh rah-zoo-MEHM, or Ne Razumem, means I don't get it.

Slovenia Travel Guide 2024

Favorite angleško, Ali? Do you know how to say "AH-lee goh-voh-REE-teh angle-shkoh?" in English?

Yes, da (dah)

Neh (neh) – No

Asking for Directions and Assistance

What does Kako pridem do? (Pree-DEHM doh KAH-koh...) How can I arrive at...?

Kje je...? (Kyeh yeh...) In what location is...?

Desno (DEHS-noh) – Left Naravnost (NAH-rahv-nost) – Right Levo (LEH-voh) - Unwavering

Before me, or pred mano (prehd MAH-noh)

Za mano, which translates to "behind me,"

Next to me, Zraven Mene (zrah-VEHN meh-neh)

How do you propose to help me? (Proh-seem lah-koh mee poh-mah-GAH-teh?) Would you kindly assist me?

Potrebujem dobroč (poh-treh-boo-yem poh-moch): I require assistance.

Shopping and Ordering Food

Tokoliko stane to? (STAH-neh toh KOH-lee-koh?) What is the cost of this?

"Bi rad/a" (bee rahd/ah...) means "I want to"...

Ena. (EH-nah) Three Prosim za račun (PROH-seem zah rah-choon): One Dva (dvah): Two Tri (tree) Please give me the bill.

Please go. Hrana za s seboj (HRAH-nah zah seh-boy)

Emergency Words

Pomoč! Poh-MOCH: Assistance!

I'm calling the police, or kličem policijo (KLEE-chem poh-lee-TSI-yah).

KLEE-chem reh-SHEEL-tsah, Kličem rešilca, I'm phoning an ambulance..

I require a doctor. Potrebujem zdravnika (poh-treh-boo-yem zdrahv-NEE-kah).

I'm lost, Izgubljen/a sem (eez-goo-BLYEN/ah sem).

Etiquette and cultural norms

Salutations and social exchanges

▪ **Salutations:** Traditionally, Slovenians extend a handshake and say "živjo" (zhee-vyoh) or "Zdravo" (zdrah-vo), which translates to "hello." An embrace or a kiss on both cheeks might be given to those who are closer.

▪ **Titles:** Referencing people by their titles and surnames is suitable in formal situations. For instance, "Gospod" (pronounced goh-spohd), "Gospodična" (pronounced goh-spohd-chee-nah) for Miss, and "Gospa" (pronounced goh-spah) for Mrs.

▪ **Conversational Etiquette:** In general, Slovenians value courteous and considerate dialogue. Refrain from shouting angrily or raising your voice. Make sure you look them in the eye and pay close attention when they talk.

Dining Etiquette

Proper table manners are highly valued by Slovenians. Remain upright, use cutlery appropriately, and keep your elbows off the table. It is considered impolite to begin dining before all guests have been served.

- **Toasting:** In Slovenia, toasting is customary. To toast someone, lift your glass, meet their eyes, and say "Na zdravje" (nah zdrav-yeh), which translates to "to your health."

- **Tipping:** Although not required, it is traditional to leave a modest gratuity for excellent service or to round up the amount in Slovenia. A five- to ten-percent tip is deemed appropriate.

Public Etiquette

Slovenians usually wear modest clothing that is appropriate for the situation. Jeans and t-shirts are appropriate in casual situations, but formal settings call for dress clothing.

- **Smoking:** It is not permitted to smoke indoors in public areas, such as eateries, pubs, and cultural institutions. Smoking is permitted in specific outdoor spaces.

- **Respecting Public Spaces:** Try not to disrupt other people in public areas by being aware of noise levels. Maintain public spaces neat and orderly, and dispose of trash appropriately.

Cultural norms and sensitivities

▪ **Respect for Diversity:** There are many different cultural and ethnic groups living in Slovenia. Respect other people's cultures and customs by abstaining from generalizations and offensive language.

▪ **Environmental Consciousness:** Littering is severely forbidden in Slovenia since the people there care about the environment. Respect the nation's natural beauty and dispose of rubbish in an appropriate manner.

▪ **Respect for Regional Customs:** Invest some time in becoming knowledgeable about and appreciative of regional traditions and customs. To learn more about Slovenian culture, interact with locals, sample traditional foods, and attend cultural events.

CHAPTER NINE - SAFETY AND HEALTH IN SLOVENIA

Emergency Information

- Emergency phone numbers
- Emergency Services: 112 (Fire, Ambulance, Police).
- Non-emergency police: 113
- Mountain Rescue Service: 110

Medical Care

In case of an emergency, dial 112 to get help right away.

- **Hospitals:** The healthcare system in Slovenia is well developed, and the nation is home to a large number of hospitals. Major hospitals with specialized care can be found in larger cities like Maribor and Ljubljana.

- **Pharmacies:** In both towns and villages, pharmacies are easily accessible. Usually open from

8:00 a.m. to 6:00 p.m., they could be closed on weekends.

Transportation

Roadside help and vehicle breakdowns can be arranged by calling AMZS (Auto-moto Zveza Slovenije) in 1987. They offer towing and roadside assistance around the clock.

▪ **Train Cancellations or Delays:** Call Slovenske Železnice (SŽ) at +386 1 2005 111 for information on train cancellations or delays. They offer up-to-date information on delays and schedules for trains.

▪ **Road Closures and Traffic Disruptions:** Check the website or mobile app of the Slovenian Traffic Information Centre (PROMET) for information on road closures and traffic disruptions. They offer information on road conditions and traffic updates in real time.

Generally Speaking

▪ **Crime Rates:** Although there isn't much crime in Slovenia, it's still a good idea to exercise common-sense caution and never carry large sums of cash or valuables in public. Be mindful of your surroundings and take care of your belongings.

▪ **Natural Disasters:** Occasionally, events like earthquakes and floods can cause havoc in Slovenia. In the event of an emergency, be aware of the possible hazards and heed the local safety advice.

▪ **Travel Insurance:** Before visiting Slovenia, it is advised that you get travel insurance. Loss of luggage, medical bills, and trip cancellations can all be covered by travel insurance.

Extra Materials

▪ **Tourist Information:** Travel plans, attractions, events, and emergency assistance are all covered in detail on Slovenia's official tourism website, slovenia.info.

▪ **Embassies and Consulates:** In the event of an emergency, foreign nationals should get in touch with the embassy or consulate of their home nation in Slovenia.

Health Precautions

Vaccinations

- **Regular Immunizations:** Verify that you have received all recommended immunizations, including those for polio, tetanus, diphtheria, and pertussis (Tdap), measles, mumps, and rubella (MMR), and others.

- **Suggested Immunizations:** Take into account receiving vaccinations against rabies, tick-borne encephalitis (TBE), hepatitis A and B, and hepatitis B, depending on your travel plans and activities. To find out which vaccinations are advised for your travel, speak with your doctor.

Insect Defense

- **Encephalitis** caused by ticks in forested environments is known as tick-borne encephalitis (TBE). It is advised that visitors to rural areas who intend to engage in outdoor activities such as trekking or camping get vaccinated against TBE.

- **Mosquitoes and Lyme Disease**: Mosquitoes can transmit Lyme disease in some parts of Slovenia. Use insect repellent containing DEET or picaridin when spending time outdoors, especially in wooded areas. Wear long-sleeved shirts and pants to further reduce mosquito exposure.

Sun Protection

Sunburn is a possibility in Slovenia due to its sunny weather and steep terrain. Use sunglasses, sunscreen with an SPF of 30 or higher, and seek shade during the hottest parts of the day to protect yourself from the sun's harmful rays.

Food and water safety

▪ **Drinking Water:** In Slovenia, tap water is usually safe to consume. But if you're worried, especially in rural regions, think about drinking bottled water.

▪ **Food Safety:** To lower your chance of contracting a foodborne illness, stay away from raw or undercooked meat, fish, and eggs. When it comes to eating street cuisine, stay with respectable establishments and vendors and exercise caution.

General health advice

▪ **Essential Medication Pack:** Don't forget to pack over-the-counter prescriptions for common conditions, including headaches, upset stomachs, and allergies, in addition to any prescription medications you frequently take.

▪ **Keep Yourself Hydrated:** Throughout the day, especially in warm weather or when exercising, sip lots of water.

▪ **Keep Your Diet Healthy:** Whenever possible, go for fresh, locally sourced food. Steer clear of consuming too much alcohol, sugary drinks, and processed food.

▪ **Seek Medical Attention When Necessary:** If you become ill while traveling, don't be afraid to get medical help. Slovenia's healthcare system is well-equipped, and access to medical care is easy.

CHAPTER TEN - TIPS FOR RESPONSIBLE TRAVEL TO SLOVENIA

Eco-friendly Practice in Slovenia

Recycling and waste handling

Slovenia has a well-functioning waste management system that prioritizes recycling and minimizing trash. The nation's recycling rates for municipal waste are remarkable, surpassing the EU average.

▪ **Multi-bin System:** Slovenia has a multi-bin system for home garbage that encourages citizens to segregate various waste materials for effective recycling, including paper, plastic, glass, and organic waste.

▪ **Recycling Infrastructure:** Slovenians may easily recycle their waste thanks to the country's well-established network of recycling facilities and pickup sites.

▪ **Facilities for Composting:** Slovenia encourages composting as an environmentally friendly method of handling organic waste. Many local governments encourage citizens to compost at home or provide composting sites.

Green Mobility and Transportation

Slovenia is aggressively pushing environmentally friendly modes of transportation in an effort to lessen its dependency on fossil fuels and enhance air quality.

▪ **Public transit system:** trains, buses, and trams are all part of Slovenia's well-established and effective public transit system. Both locals and guests can access convenient and reasonably priced transit choices through this network.

Slovenia is making investments in bike infrastructure, including the construction of bike lanes and walkways, in an effort to promote riding as a means of transportation.

▪ **Electric Mobility**: Slovenia is promoting the adoption of electric vehicles by providing subsidies and incentives for purchasing electric cars and installing charging stations.

Ecotourism and sustainable travel

In an effort to reduce its influence on the environment and encourage responsible travel, Slovenia's tourist sector is adopting sustainable practices.

Slovenia has put in place the Green Scheme of Slovenian Tourism, a certification program that honors and promotes travel companies that are dedicated to sustainability.

▪ **Experiences with Ecotourism:** Slovenia has a range of ecotourism activities, including hiking in national parks, going to eco-friendly farms, and looking into sustainable lodging options.

▪ **Campaigns for Environmental Awareness:** Slovenia encourages responsible behavior in natural areas and runs educational campaigns to raise awareness of environmental issues among tourists.

Efficiency in Energy Use and Renewable Energy

Slovenia is dedicated to using more renewable energy sources and consuming less energy overall.

Slovenia has enacted legislation pertaining to energy efficiency for both buildings and appliances, with the aim of encouraging the adoption of energy-efficient technologies.

Slovenia is making investments in renewable energy sources, like geothermal, wind, and solar electricity, in an effort to lessen its reliance on fossil fuels.

- **Sustainable Energy for Public Buildings:** Slovenia is giving renewable energy sources top priority when it comes to public buildings, including hospitals, schools, and government offices.

Respect for the local community

Traveling responsibly requires respecting the locals, which makes your trip to Slovenia more enjoyable overall. During your travels, remember to take the following important measures to show respect for the local community:

1. Accept Local Customs and Traditions: The people of Slovenia are strongly rooted in a range of customs and traditions that are part of their rich cultural heritage. Learn as much as you can about these traditions and customs, and try to follow them with courtesy. This enhances the immersion of the vacation experience and demonstrates respect for the native way of life.

2. Support Local Businesses: Give preference to small, locally owned businesses over national chains when making purchases or requesting services. This creates a more genuine experience, boosts the local economy, and preserves traditional crafts and skills. Talk to the local retailers and craftspeople, discover more about their offerings, and value the handcrafted nature of their creations.

3. Show Respect for the Environment: Slovenia is well known for its breathtakingly beautiful scenery, which includes majestic mountains, pure lakes, and charming scenery. Handle these natural gems with respect. Refrain from littering, properly dispose of rubbish, and do not harm wildlife or vegetation. Give the natural world back to its original state so that future generations can continue to appreciate its splendor.

4. Be Aware of Noise Levels: Pay attention to noise levels, particularly in residential areas and late at night, to preserve the peace and quiet of nearby communities. Steer clear of boisterous discussions, loud music or car exhaust, and disruptive conduct that could annoy nearby homes.

5. Communicate with Respect: Speak to locals in a courteous and respectful manner. Acquire a few fundamental Slovenian phrases to demonstrate your desire to interact and communicate with the community. When conversing, exercise patience and refrain from assuming anything about the people or culture of the area.

6. Respect Private Property: Show consideration for private property by not entering buildings or trespassing on private property. When touring the countryside, stay on established routes and paths and stay out of people's yards and gardens.

7. Dress Respectfully: Although Slovenians like to dress casually, it's always a good idea to show consideration for local populations, particularly when visiting places that are conservative or religious. Steer clear of anything too revealing or perhaps insulting.

8. Recognize Local Work: Slovenia has achieved great progress in safeguarding its environment, encouraging sustainable practices, and maintaining its cultural legacy. Participate in cultural events, lend support to local projects, and exercise caution when traveling to show your appreciation for these efforts.

CONCLUSION

Situated in Central Europe, Slovenia is a small nation. Italy borders it on the southwest, Austria on the north, Hungary on the northeast, and Croatia on the southeast. Slovenia is a party to both the North Atlantic Treaty Organization (NATO) and the European Union. It's a developed nation with excellent living standards. Manufacturing, tourism, and services form the foundation of the economy. Slovenia is a stunning nation with a vibrant past and present. It has a large number of lakes, mountains, and woods. Slovenia is a well-liked travel destination with a reputation for its hiking, snowboarding, and skiing.

Visit the capital city of Ljubljana, a charming city with a medieval center and a lively atmosphere; hike in the Julian Alps, a beautiful mountain range with stunning views; take a boat trip on Lake Bled, a picturesque lake with a small island in the middle; or pay a visit to the Predjama Castle, a 13th-century castle built into a cliff. Slovenia is a country that has a lot to offer visitors. It is a beautiful country with a rich history and culture. It is also a safe and friendly nation with a high standard of living. In the winter, go skiing or snowboarding; in the summer, go bicycling or hiking.

Printed in Great Britain
by Amazon

40625344R00056